GREATEST OF ALL TIME COLLEGE SPORTS

G.O.A.T. COLLEGE WOMEN'S BASKETBALL PLAYERS

Diane Lindsey Reeves

Lerner Publications ◆ Minneapolis

Special thanks to my favorite college women's basketball fans, Gayle Lindsey Bryan and Hollis Grace Palmer.

Stats in this book are accurate through the 2023–2024 women's college basketball season.

Lerner Publications Company
An imprint of Lerner Publishing Group, Inc.
241 First Avenue North
Minneapolis, MN 55401 USA

For reading levels and more information, look up this title at www.lernerbooks.com.

Main body text set in Aptifer Sans LT Pro.
Typeface provided by Linotype.

Library of Congress Cataloging-in-Publication Data

Names: Reeves, Diane Lindsey, 1959–author.
Title: G.O.A.T. college women's basketball players / Diane Lindsey Reeves.
Other titles: GOAT college women's basketball players
Description: Minneapolis, MN : Lerner Publications, 2025. | Series: Greatest of all time college sports (Lerner sports) | Includes bibliographical references and index. | Audience: Ages 7–11 | Audience: Grades 2–3 | Summary: "Caitlin Clark and other superstar players have helped women's college basketball explode in popularity in recent years. Meet the greatest players of all time, review their stats, and then choose your top ten"—Provided by publisher.
Identifiers: LCCN 2024051092 (print) | LCCN 2024051093 (ebook) | ISBN 9798765668597 (library binding) | ISBN 9798765684214 (paperback) | ISBN 9798765677896 (epub)
Subjects: LCSH: Basketball players—Rating of—United States—Juvenile literature. | Women basketball players—Rating of—United States—Juvenile literature. | College athletes—Rating of—United States—Juvenile literature. | Women college athletes—Rating of—United States—Juvenile literature. | College sports—Juvenile literature. | Basketball—United States—History—Juvenile literature.
Classification: LCC GV885.1 .R428 2025 (print) | LCC GV885.1 (ebook) | DDC 796.323092/520973—dc23/eng/20250129

LC record available at https://lccn.loc.gov/2024051092
LC ebook record available at https://lccn.loc.gov/2024051093

Manufactured in the United States of America
1-1011970-53827-4/24/2025

TABLE OF CONTENTS

WOMEN PLAY TO WIN 4

No. 10 Sheryl Swoopes 8

No. 9 A'ja Wilson 10

No. 8 Caitlin Clark 12

No. 7 Nancy Lieberman 14

No. 6 Maya Moore 16

No. 5 Candace Parker 18

No. 4 Lisa Leslie 20

No. 3 Brittney Griner 22

No. 2 Cheryl Miller 24

No. 1 Breanna Stewart 26

Your G.O.A.T. 28

Women's College Basketball Facts 29

Glossary 30

Learn More 31

Index 32

Players such as Iowa's Caitlin Clark (right) raise the bar for female basketball players.

Women Play to Win

Women's college basketball has come a long way since it started in 1893. In the first game, sophomores at Smith College took on the freshmen. The women wore long skirts. No men were allowed to watch the game.

Women playing basketball was a wild idea at the time. Some people thought women players would get hurt or tire more easily than men. Men's basketball rules were changed for women. The women's game was played in two 15-minute halves. Players had to pass the ball after only three dribbles. Each basket counted for one point.

College basketball legend Cheryl Miller helped make women's basketball popular with fans.

FACTS AT A GLANCE

- Sheryl Swoopes was the first women's basketball player to have a Nike shoe named after her. Air Swoopes first hit store shelves in 1995.
- Brittney Griner is the only NCAA player to score at least 2,000 points and block at least 500 shots in her career.
- Breanna Stewart is the only college player to block at least 400 shots and have 400 or more assists.
- In 2024, Caitlin Clark became the all-time leading scorer in NCAA basketball history. She passed the record set by Pete Maravich in 1970.

In modern women's basketball, games are fast and rough. Athletes are skilled, well-trained, and always setting new records. Some players, such as Caitlin Clark, are smashing long-held records of both men and women. Ticket prices for the women's 2024 National College Athletic Association (NCAA) Final Four games were twice as high as prices for the men's games.

Much credit for the popularity of college women's basketball is also due to other players. Exciting stars such as Cheryl Miller, Candace Parker, and Sheryl Swoopes helped make women's basketball popular. They inspired generations of young women to bring their best to the court.

Limiting this greatest of all time (G.O.A.T.) list of women college players to only 10 was tough. The players who made it were chosen for their stats, awards, and the ways they made basketball better. Your list may be different. You'll have a chance to make your own G.O.A.T. list at the end of the book. Who will make it, and who won't?

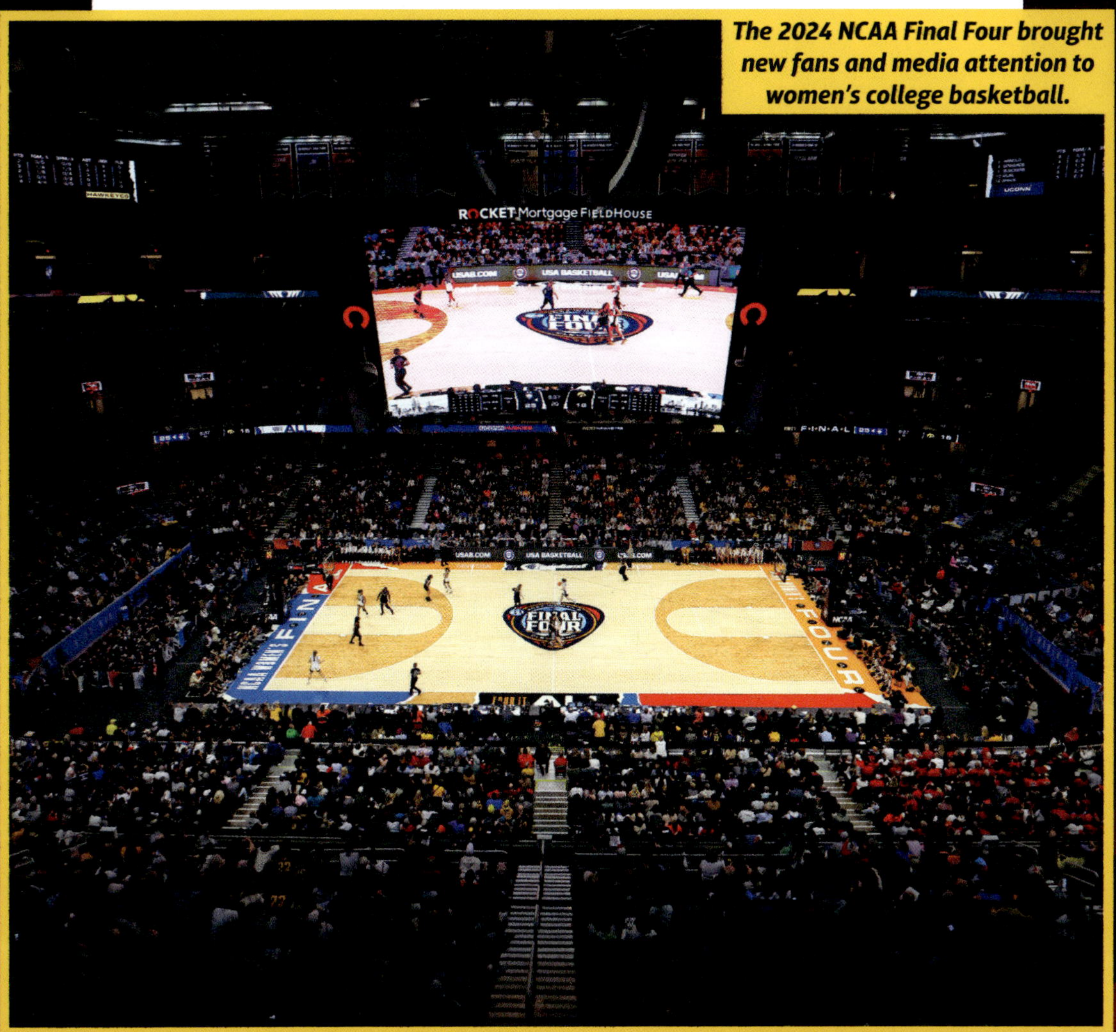

The 2024 NCAA Final Four brought new fans and media attention to women's college basketball.

No. 10

Hall of Famer Sheryl Swoopes led her team to an NCAA title win in 1993.

Sheryl Swoopes

Texas Tech University (1991–1993)

Sheryl Swoopes had a career full of wins and honors at Texas Tech University. But one game shines especially bright. It was the 1993 NCAA title game against Ohio State. Swoopes led her team to an 84–82 win by scoring 47 points. She set a points record for an NCAA title game.

The win against Ohio State topped off an amazing senior year for Swoopes. She scored 955 points during the 1992–1993 season. Her 24.9 points-per-game average is the best in school history.

During her college career, Swoopes racked up three triple-doubles and 23 double-doubles. Her amazing college stats, plus her starring role as a WNBA player, explain why she is in the Naismith Memorial Basketball Hall of Fame.

Swoopes won her first gold medal with the US Olympic team in 1996.

SHERYL SWOOPES FACTS

- **In the 1993 NCAA title game, Swoopes missed only eight shots. Her total of 47 points is 16 more than any other player has scored in the title game.**
- **When the WNBA started in 1997, Swoopes played for the Houston Comets. She was the first Black woman to sign a WNBA contract.**
- **Swoopes played on the US Olympic women's basketball team and won gold medals in 1996, 2000, and 2004.**
- **Swoopes was the first female basketball player to have Nike shoes named after her. Air Swoopes sold from 1995 to 2002. The shoes made a comeback in 2018.**

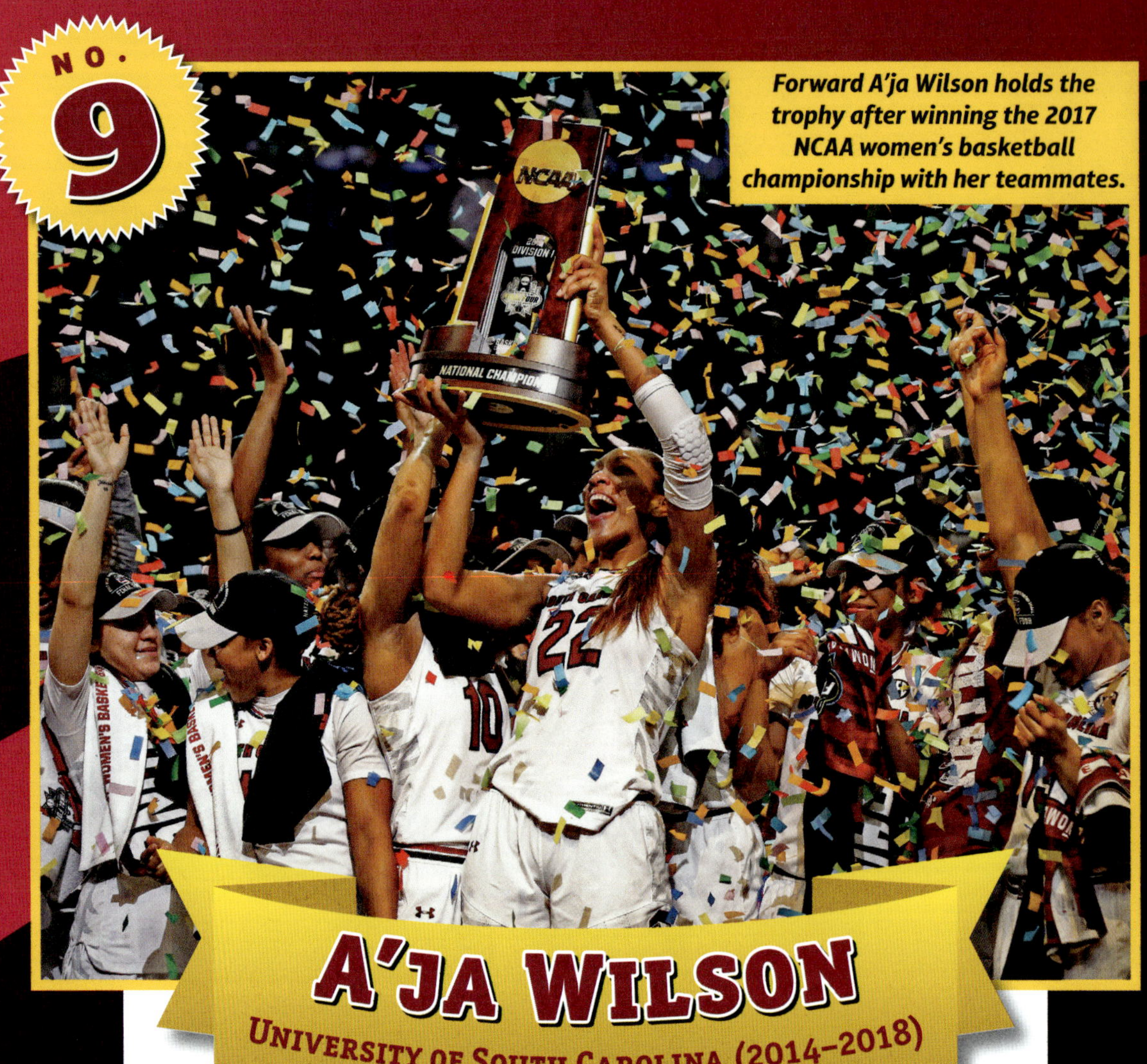

NO. 9

Forward A'ja Wilson holds the trophy after winning the 2017 NCAA women's basketball championship with her teammates.

A'JA WILSON

UNIVERSITY OF SOUTH CAROLINA (2014–2018)

A'ja Wilson was strong on both offense and defense at the University of South Carolina. Opponents guarded her every move, but she still managed to dominate. Starting her freshman season, she was in the top 10 in the US in double-doubles, scoring, rebounding, and blocked shots per game.

Over four years, she racked up an impressive list of honors, awards, and trophies. In her senior year at South Carolina, she was named National Player of the Year by top sports news groups such as ESPN and *USA Today*. She was the Southeastern Conference Player of the Year three times.

In 2017, Wilson and coach Dawn Staley led South Carolina to their first NCAA title. In the final game, they beat Mississippi State 67–55. Wilson came through for her team in a big way. She had 23 points, 10 rebounds, and four blocked shots in the game.

A'ja Wilson* (right) *blocks a shot against the Stanford Cardinal in 2017.

A'JA WILSON FACTS

- **Wilson set South Carolina career records with 2,389 points, 363 blocked shots, and 597 free throws made.**
- **In her senior year, Wilson was the only player to rank in the top 35 in the US in scoring, rebounding, and blocking shots.**
- **To honor Wilson, a statue of the star player stands near the main entrance to South Carolina's basketball arena.**
- **She wrote the book *Dear Black Girls: How to Be True to You*, in 2024.**

NO. 8

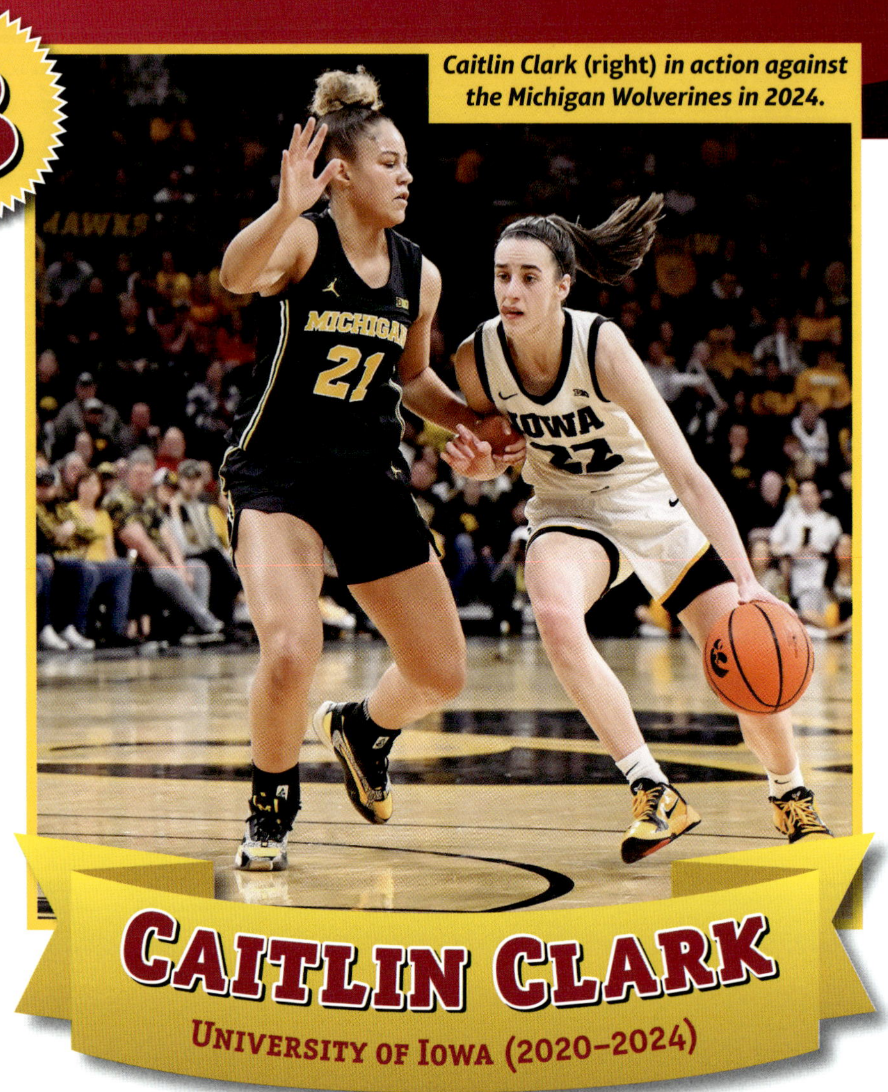

Caitlin Clark (right) in action against the Michigan Wolverines in 2024.

CAITLIN CLARK

UNIVERSITY OF IOWA (2020–2024)

Caitlin Clark is best known for shattering NCAA and Big Ten Conference records. In her four years at Iowa, she scored more points than any other men's or women's college player. Her total of 3,951 career points crushed the all-time NCAA record of 3,667 set by Pete Maravich in 1970.

No one shot three-pointers like Clark. In her senior year, she hit 201 three-point baskets. She finished her career with a record-breaking 548 three-pointers. In 2023, she set another record with eight three-pointers in the NCAA women's title game. Iowa lost to Louisiana State 102–85.

Clark's last college game was the 2024 NCAA title game against South Carolina. More than 18 million fans watched her last chance to win a national title. It was the biggest TV audience ever for a women's game. South Carolina beat Iowa 87–75. But Clark went out with a bang. Her 18 points in the first quarter broke another NCAA record.

Clark* (right) *shoots another three-pointer in a game against the West Virginia Mountaineers in 2024.

CAITLIN CLARK FACTS

- Clark's grandfather, father, brother, and two uncles were college athletes. Her grandfather later became a football coach at the high school Clark attended.
- In her college career, Clark scored 40 points in a game 13 times and 30 points 59 times.
- Clark was the first men's or women's Division I player to score 3,000 or more points, at least 900 assists, and 800 or more rebounds in a college career.
- She averaged 28.4 points per game to set another women's NCAA basketball record.

NO. 7

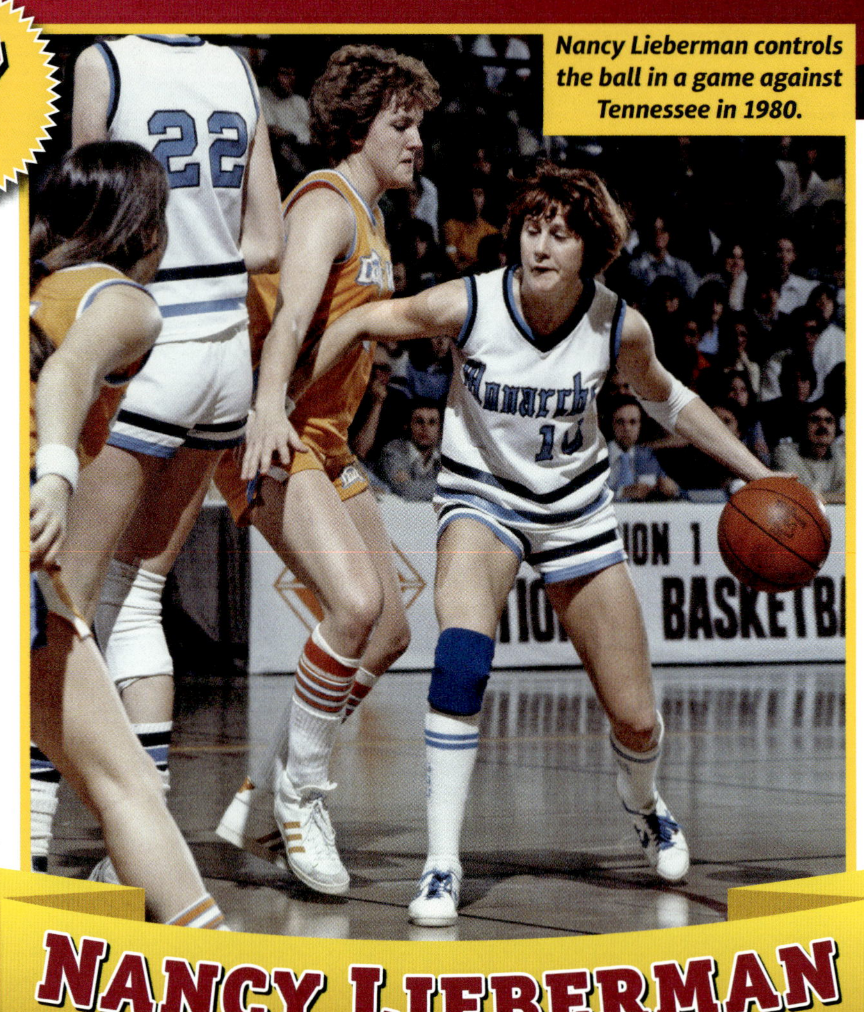

Nancy Lieberman controls the ball in a game against Tennessee in 1980.

NANCY LIEBERMAN

OLD DOMINION UNIVERSITY (1976–1980)

Point guard Nancy Lieberman was an all-around amazing basketball player. She was skilled at driving the ball to the hoop, grabbing rebounds, and making assists. She won awards as the nation's top women's player in 1979 and 1980. Lieberman played for Old Dominion before NCAA tournaments started. But she still led her team to national titles in her final two years of college.

She earned the nickname Lady Magic in part because of her assists. In her sophomore year, Lieberman averaged 8.9 assists per game. With a career total of 961 assists, she set a school record that still stands. She also set a record by making more than 75 percent of her free throws.

Lieberman* (second from left) *was one of the first women to coach a pro men's basketball team.

The many awards Lieberman won tell the story of her college basketball greatness. She was the first player to win two Wade Trophies. That award goes to the best NCAA women's basketball player.

NANCY LIEBERMAN FACTS

- In a game against Norfolk State in 1977, Lieberman scored a triple-double with 40 points, 15 rebounds, and 11 assists.
- Lieberman set a school record by stealing the ball 562 times during her career.
- She was the second woman in history to coach a pro men's team. She was an assistant coach for the NBA's Sacramento Kings in 2015.
- Every year, the Nancy Lieberman Award honors the top point guard in women's NCAA Division I basketball.

NO. 6

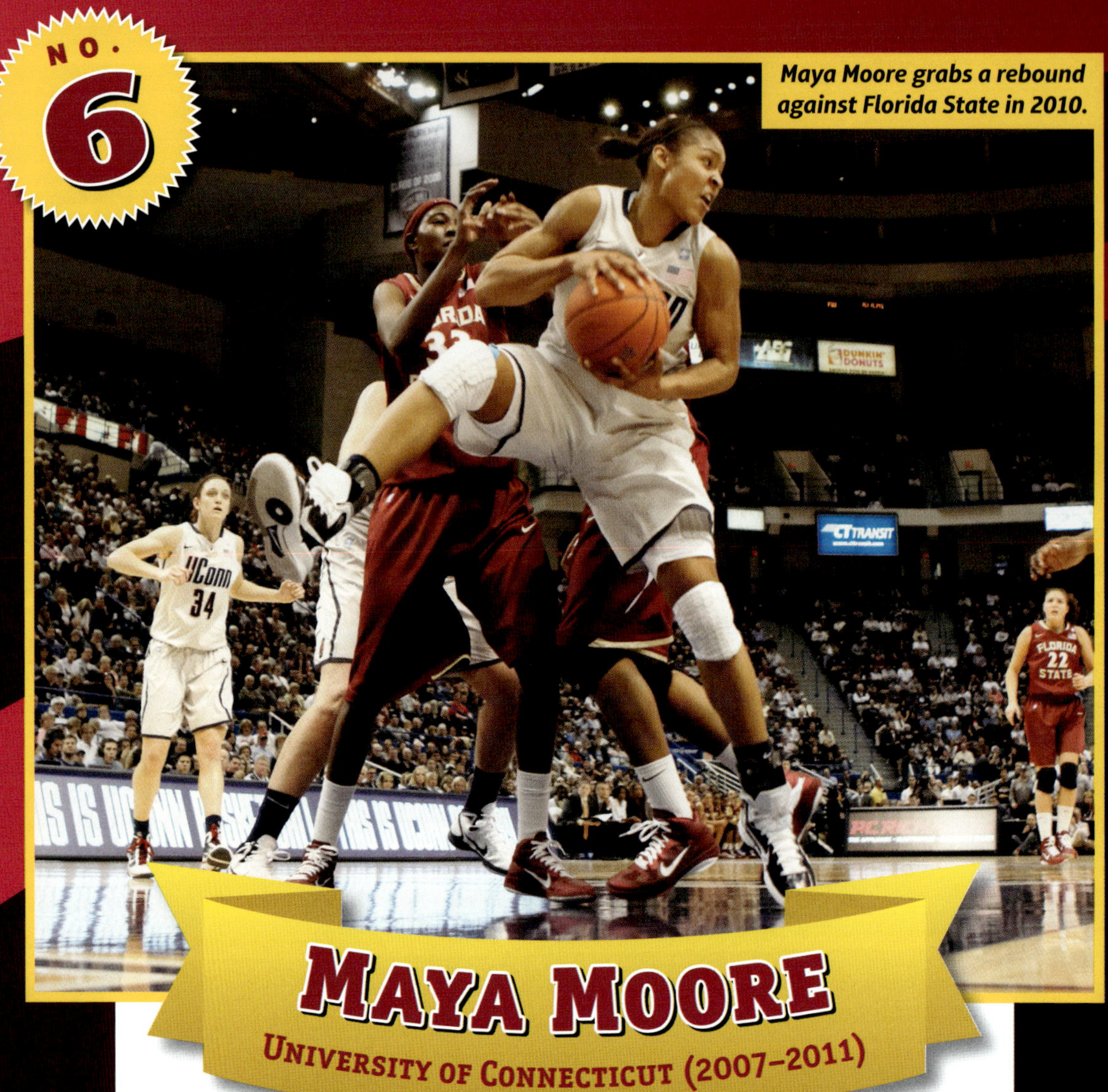

Maya Moore grabs a rebound against Florida State in 2010.

MAYA MOORE

UNIVERSITY OF CONNECTICUT (2007–2011)

Forward Maya Moore was one of the winningest players in NCAA history. She led the University of Connecticut (UConn) to 150 wins and only four losses over her college career. Her team made it to the NCAA Final Four every year she played.

UConn won back-to-back NCAA titles in 2009 and 2010. Both titles came after undefeated seasons. And Moore was a major force behind the team's 90-game winning streak that began in 2008 and didn't end until December 2010.

Moore finished as one of college women's basketball's highest scorers with 3,036 career points. She scored at least 10 points in a record-breaking 149 games. She is one of only two players to be an AP First Team All-American all four years of college. *Sports Illustrated* called her the greatest winner in the history of women's basketball.

UConn's Maya Moore makes a basket against Stanford in an NCAA Women's Final Four game.

MAYA MOORE FACTS

- Before starring for UConn, Moore was already a standout player. In high school, she won the National Gatorade Player of the Year award, the Gatorade Female Athlete of the Year award, and a McDonald's All-American honor.
- Moore scored 30 points for the sixth time in her college career in a 65–64 win over Baylor in 2011. She also tied her career high of six steals.
- Moore was the number-one pick in the 2011 WNBA draft. She played for the Minnesota Lynx for eight seasons and won four championships.
- Moore joined the Women's Basketball Hall of Fame in 2024.

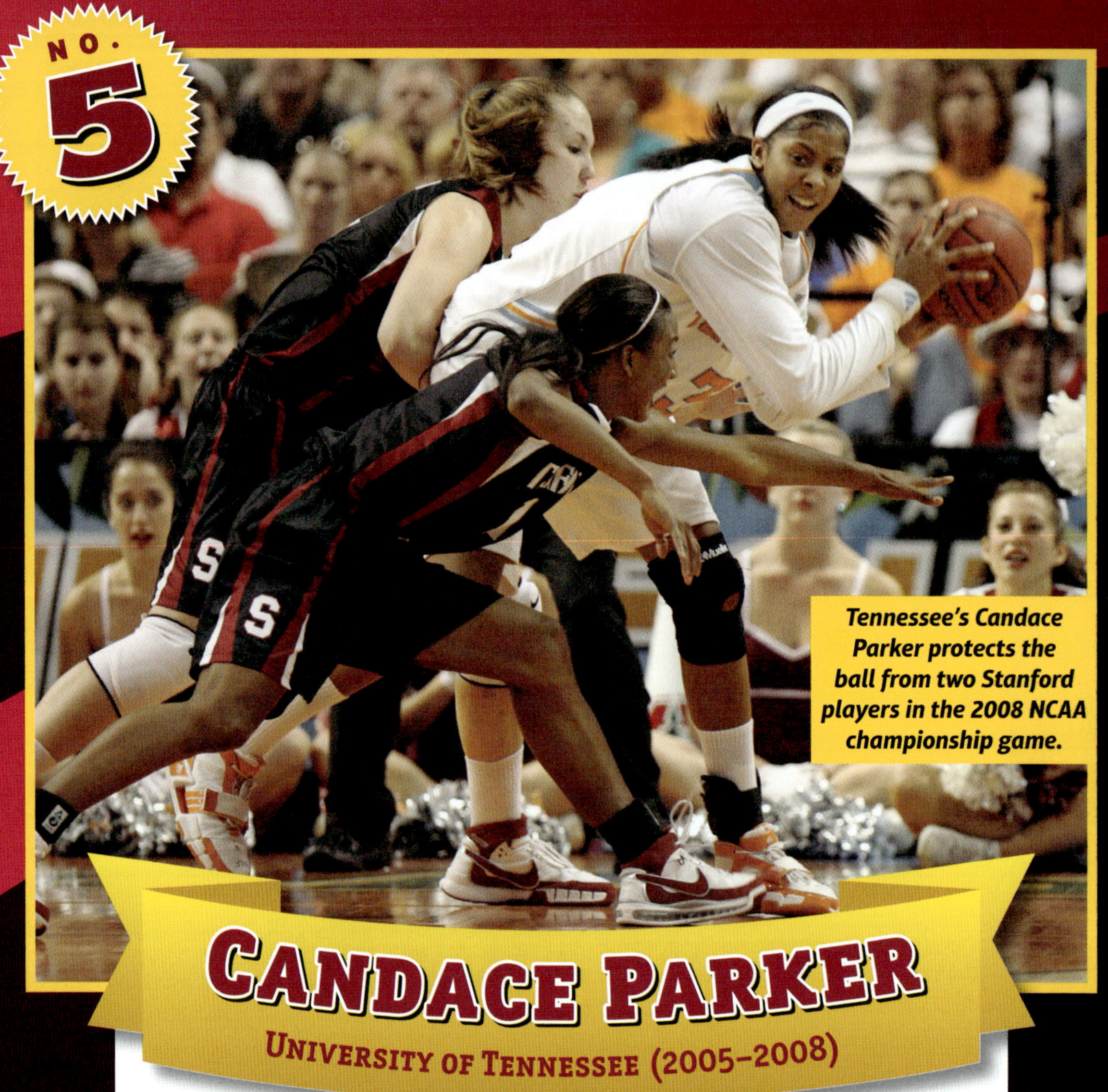

Tennessee's Candace Parker protects the ball from two Stanford players in the 2008 NCAA championship game.

CANDACE PARKER

UNIVERSITY OF TENNESSEE (2005–2008)

Candace Parker played forward, center, and guard for Tennessee. She racked up points and assists on one end of the court and rebounds on the other. It was tough for opponents to keep up with her. She brought energy and excitement to all her games.

Parker played even better under pressure. In the 2008 NCAA championship game against Stanford, she played with an injured shoulder. But she came through with 17 points and nine rebounds to help her team win.

During her 56th college game, Parker reached the 1,000-point mark. That's the fastest any woman at Tennessee has reached this goal. Parker's leadership and skill led Tennessee to back-to-back NCAA titles in 2007 and 2008. In both years she won the Naismith College Player of the Year award.

Parker* (left) *jumps for the opening tip in the 2008 title game against Stanford.

CANDACE PARKER FACTS

- Parker was the Gatorade Girls High School Player of the Year in 2003 and 2004. She is the only girls' basketball player to win two years in a row.
- In high school, Parker won the slam dunk contest at the 2004 McDonald's All-American game. She was the first girl to win. She beat out future NBA players J. R. Smith, Rudy Gay, and Josh Smith.
- In 2006, Parker became the first woman to dunk the ball in an NCAA tournament game. She was also the first women's player to dunk twice in a college game.

No. 4

Lisa Leslie prepares to shoot a free throw against the University of Virginia Cavaliers in 1991.

Lisa Leslie

University of Southern California (1990–1994)

Lisa Leslie's college career got off to a strong start at the University of Southern California (USC). She was the Pac-10 Conference Rookie of the Year and National Freshman of the Year in 1991. She was still going strong in 1994 when she led her team to a conference title.

In her senior year, she was the Naismith College Player of the Year. Leslie was the first player in Pac-10 history to make the All-Pac-10 team four times. Along the way, Leslie led her team to four NCAA tournament appearances.

She finished with an average of 20.1 points per game in 120 college games. She hit 53.4 percent of her shots and 69.8 percent of her free throws. She is remembered for her grace as a player as well as her strength and skill.

Lisa Leslie was honored by the US Olympic Hall of Fame in 2019.

LISA LESLIE FACTS

- In high school, Leslie scored 101 points during the first half of a game.
- Leslie set Pac-10 Conference records for scoring (2,414), rebounding (1,214), and blocked shots (321).
- Leslie won gold medals with the USA Olympic team in 1996, 2000, 2004, and 2008. She set a US Olympic record in 1996 by scoring 35 points against Japan.
- In 2024, ESPN named Leslie one of the 100 greatest athletes of the 21st century.

NO. 3

In 2024, Baylor honored Brittney Griner (right) by retiring her jersey number.

BRITTNEY GRINER

BAYLOR UNIVERSITY (2009–2013)

At 6 feet 9 (2 m), Brittney Griner towered over most other players. If her size didn't impress opponents, her power on the court did. By the end of her career at Baylor, she had scored 3,283 points and broken several records.

In her freshman year of 2009, Griner scored Baylor's first triple-double. She had 34 points, 13 rebounds, and 11 blocked shots in a game against Oral Roberts. She blocked 223 shots for the season.

With 18 slam dunks, Griner has the most career dunks in women's college basketball. She's the only college player to score at least 2,000 points and have 500 or more blocked shots. And her 748 blocks are the most in women's or men's college basketball.

In 2012, Griner led Baylor to the school's first NCAA title. She was the Naismith College Player of the Year in 2012 and 2013. She also won the Wooden Award for the best US player both years. Baylor retired her jersey number in 2024. To honor Griner, no other Baylor women's player will wear number 42.

Brittney Griner dunks the ball during warm-ups before a game against Oral Roberts University in 2012.

BRITTNEY GRINER FACTS

- Griner was already showing her athletic skills in grade school. She won two football Punt, Pass, and Kick contests.
- Griner grew up in Houston, Texas. In her senior year of high school, the mayor of Houston declared May 7, 2009, Brittney Griner Day.
- In 2010, Griner set the record for most blocked shots in a single NCAA tournament game with 14.
- She is the second-tallest player in the WNBA and wears a men's size 17 shoe. Her hands are bigger than NBA player LeBron James's hands.

NO. 2

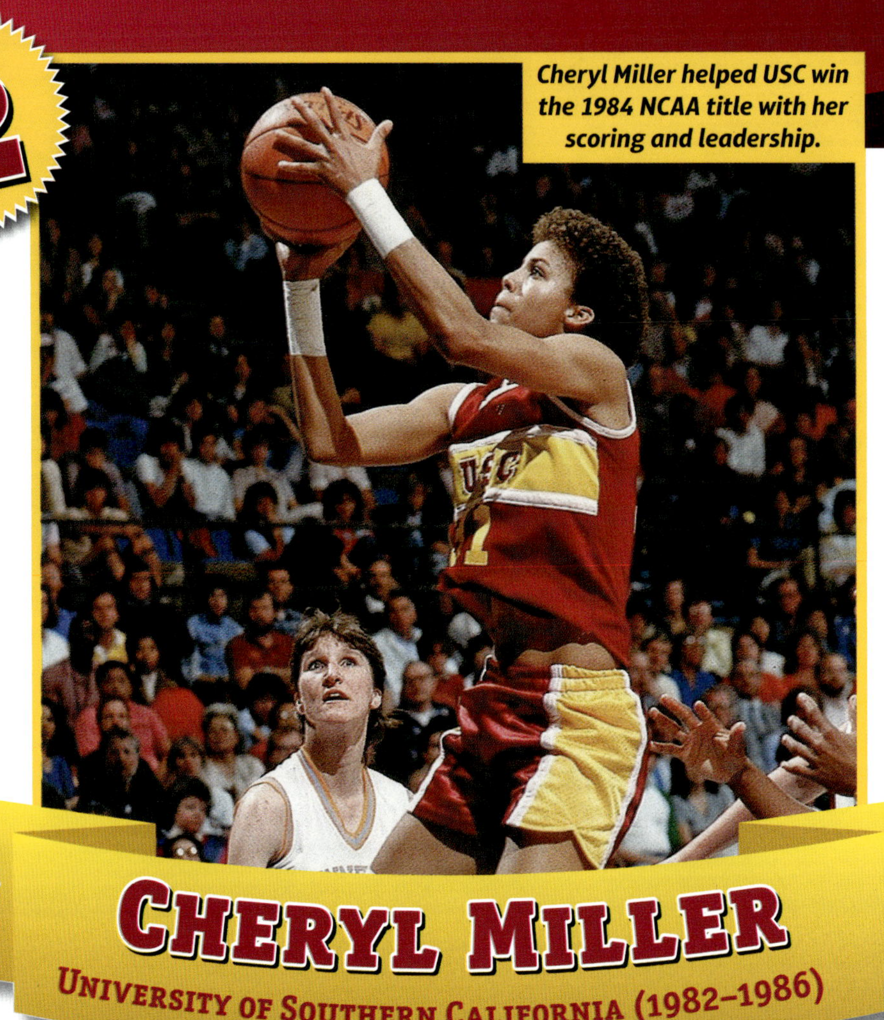

Cheryl Miller helped USC win the 1984 NCAA title with her scoring and leadership.

CHERYL MILLER

UNIVERSITY OF SOUTHERN CALIFORNIA (1982–1986)

In 1986, *Sports Illustrated* called Cheryl Miller the best player in men's and women's college basketball. She was a four-time All-American at USC. She won the Naismith Player of the Year award three times and one Wade Trophy.

Miller jumped into the spotlight as a freshman in 1982. USC won the NCAA title that season, and she won the Most Outstanding Player (MOP) award. She was a tough defender and dominant rebounder. In 1984, USC won the title and Miller was the MOP again.

By the time she graduated in 1986, she had racked up 3,018 points and 1,534 rebounds. She was the best women's basketball player in USC history. She was also the first USC player to have their jersey number retired. No other USC player wears the number 31 in honor of Miller's career.

Miller set many USC and NCAA records, including career points, rebounds, and baskets made. She still holds USC records for points, rebounds, baskets made, free throws, steals, and games played.

Cheryl Miller grabs the ball in a game against Old Dominion University in 1985.

CHERY MILLER FACTS

- Playing on the 1984 US Olympic team, Miller scored more than 16 points per game and won a gold medal.
- In 1996, Miller made history as the first woman to announce an NBA game on national TV.
- Miller returned to USC in 1993 to be head coach of the women's basketball team.
- Miller's younger brother, Reggie Miller, played for the NBA's Indiana Pacers from 1987 to 2005. He was an all-star shooting guard.

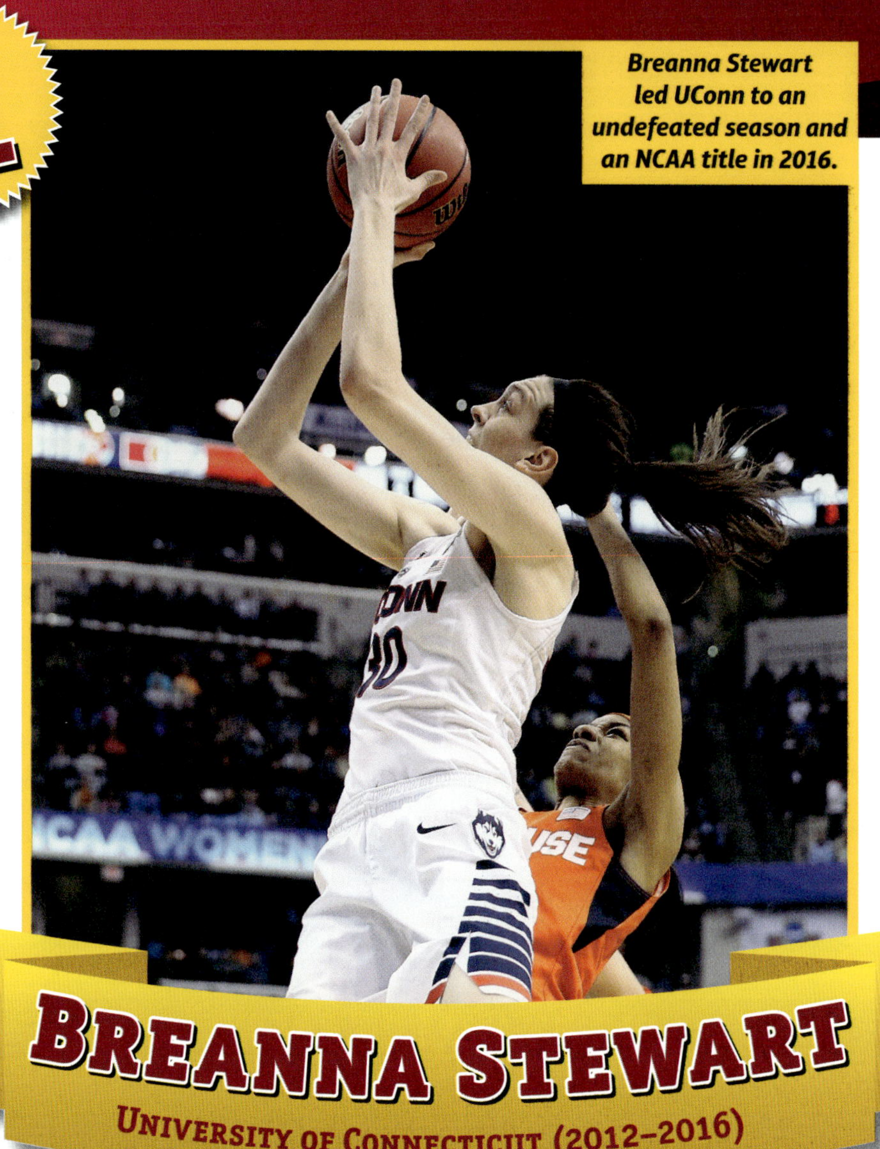

Breanna Stewart led UConn to an undefeated season and an NCAA title in 2016.

Breanna Stewart

University of Connecticut (2012–2016)

In Breanna Stewart's amazing college career, UConn had 151 wins and only five losses. In 2014 and 2016, Stewart led the team to unbeaten seasons and national titles.

UConn won the NCAA title in all four seasons Stewart played. She won the NCAA Women's Final Four MOP award four times. Stewart was also the first player to be AP Player of the Year three times.

Stewart made her mark on the court in many ways. She was an all-around player who could shoot, rebound, and defend. She set a school record for free throws in one season when she made 147 in 2013–2014.

Stewart in action during the NCAA Women's Final Four in 2015

Stewart's senior year was her best. She had 8.7 rebounds and four assists per game. She hit 57.9 percent of her shots. No one was surprised when the Seattle Storm chose Stewart with the first overall pick in the 2016 WNBA draft.

BREANNA STEWART FACTS

- In high school, Stewart worked on her dribbling skills by putting on her headphones and dribbling the ball around her neighborhood.
- She scored at least 20 points in three of her first four games as a college player. Her 169 points after 10 games broke a record held by Maya Moore.
- Stewart is the only women's college player to block at least 400 shots and have at least 400 assists.
- She won the 2016 WNBA Rookie of the Year award.

YOUR G.O.A.T.

It's your turn to put together your own list of G.O.A.T. women's college basketball players. Which players stand out as amazing to you? Who would you most like to watch play? What stats and facts will you consider when you make your list?

The players in this book were chosen by their stats, awards, and special ways they made the game better. Some are recent college players. Others made their mark on the game a long time ago. All the players except Caitlin Clark won at least one national title.

Grab a pen and a sheet of paper and make your G.O.A.T. list. Do any of your picks match the players in this book? It's your list. You decide!

WOMEN'S COLLEGE BASKETBALL FACTS

- In 1982, Drake University's Lorri Bauman scored 50 points in an 89–78 loss to Maryland in the first NCAA women's tournament. She set a record that has still not been topped. Bauman scored 64 percent of her team's points in the game.

- South Carolina coach Dawn Staley played for the University of Virginia. In 1991, she was named the MOP of the NCAA Final Four even though her team lost. She is the only player from a losing team to win the award. As a coach, she has led South Carolina's women's team to titles in 2017, 2022, and 2024.

- The balls used in women's college basketball games are 1 inch (2.5 cm) smaller than the balls used in men's games. Women's balls also weigh 2 ounces (56 g) less than men's basketballs.

GLOSSARY

conference: a group of teams that play against one another

Division I: the top level of NCAA athletics

double-double: when a player reaches at least 10 in two different stats categories in a game

draft: when teams take turns choosing new players

Final Four: the last four teams competing in the NCAA national tournament

free throw: an open shot taken from behind a set line after a foul by an opponent

National Collegiate Athletic Association (NCAA): the group that oversees college sports in the United States

rebound: grabbing and controlling the ball after a missed shot

slam dunk: a shot in basketball made by jumping high into the air and throwing the ball down through the basket

three-point shot: a shot taken from behind the three-point line on the court

title: championship

triple-double: when a player reaches at least 10 in three different stats categories in a game

WNBA: Women's National Basketball Association, the top pro league for women's basketball in the US

LEARN MORE

Brittanica Kids: Basketball
https://kids.britannica.com/kids/article/basketball/352831

Kelley, K.C. *WNBA Superstars*. Mankato, MN: The Child's World, 2020.

Kiddle: Women's Basketball Facts for Kids
https://kids.kiddle.co/Women%27s_basketball

Roggio, Sarah. *Caitlin Clark vs. Cheryl Miller: Who Would Win?* Minneapolis: Lerner Publications, 2026.

Wonderopolis: What Is March Madness?
https://www.wonderopolis.org/wonder/what-is-march-madness

Nelson, Kristen Rajczak. *Caitlin Clark: College Basketball GOAT.* Buffalo, NY: Gareth Stevens Publishing, 2025.

INDEX

Air Swoopes, 6, 9

Big Ten conference, 12

Division I, 13, 15, 30

ESPN, 11, 21

James, LeBron, 23

Nancy Lieberman Award, 15

Nike, 6, 9

Pac-10 Conference, 20–21

Pete Maravich, 6, 12

Reggie Miller, 25

Southeastern Conference, 11

Sports Illustrated, 17, 24

USA Today, 11

US Olympics, 9, 21, 25

PHOTO ACKNOWLEDGMENTS

Interior; Shutterstock/EFKS, interior; iStockphoto/robertsrob, interior; iStockphoto/9859873_183, interior; Shutterstock/yummybuum, interior; Shutterstock/AlexVoylokov, p.4; Getty/Icon Sportswire, p.5; Getty/Tony Duffy, p.7; Getty/Brendall O'Banon, p. 8; Getty/Jeff Gund, p. 9; Getty/Rick Stewart, p.10; Getty/Richard W. Rodriguez, p. 11; Getty/Ron Jenkins, p. 12; Getty/IconSportswire, p. 13; Getty/Rebecca Gratz, p. 14; Getty/George Tideman, p. 15; Getty/Icon Sportswire, p. 16; Getty/Damian Strohmeyer, p. 17; Getty/Hartford Courant, p. 18; Getty/Orlando Sentinel, p. 19; Getty/NCAA Photos, p. 20; Getty/Ken Levine, p. 21; Getty/Michael Ciaglo, p. 22; Getty/Ron Jenkins, p. 23; Getty/Cooper Neill, p. 24; Getty/Peter Read Miller, p. 25; Getty/Carl Skalak, p. 26; Getty/Andy Lyons; p. 27; Getty/Joe Robbins.

Cover: AP Images/ Carolyn Kaster